FLORIDA

STUDY GUIDE COMMUNITY HEALTH

WORKER

Dr. Dorothy Brown

LMHC, LPC, MCAP, CCHW, CMHP

Published by:

M&A Community Outreach Center, Inc.

1400 North P Street, Pensacola, FL 32505

P.O. Box 2071, Pensacola, FL 32513

For permissions and inquiries, contact:

Email: macommunity44@gmail.com

Phone: 850-429-1755

Welcome to the Florida Study Guide: Community Health Worker.

Community Health Workers (CHWs) play an indispensable role in public health, working at the heart of their communities to promote health, wellness, and equity. This guide has been thoughtfully prepared to provide CHWs in Florida with the knowledge, skills, and resources necessary to excel in their roles.

Authorship and Expertise:

This guide was developed by **Dr. Dorothy Brown**, founder of **M&A Community Outreach Center, Inc.**, a 501(c)(3) nonprofit organization committed to empowering communities since 2000. Dr. Brown brings a wealth of experience in clinical practice, counseling, and community health education to this resource.

What to Expect:

- **Foundational Knowledge:** Gain a thorough understanding of the roles, responsibilities, and ethical standards of CHWs.
- **Skill Development:** Build critical skills in communication, assessment, advocacy, and community outreach.
- **Legal and Ethical Practices:** Learn about regulations such as HIPAA, OSHA, and ADA that guide CHW practices.
- **Practical Tools:** Prepare for certification with practice questions, answers, and actionable strategies for success.

How to Use This Guide:

Each section of this guide is designed to be user-friendly and practical. Use the **Table of Contents** to locate specific topics and refer to the practice questions to test your knowledge and application of key concepts.

As you embark on this journey, remember that your work as a CHW is critical to building healthier and more equitable communities. Thank you for your dedication to this meaningful and impactful profession.

Dr. Dorothy Brown

M&A Community Outreach Center, Inc.

Table of Contents

What is a Community Health Worker (CHW)?

Community Health Workers Defined

Imagine being the bridge that connects people in need with life-changing resources—this is the role of a Community Health Worker (CHW). As a frontline public health professional, a CHW is a trusted community member who understands the people they serve on a deeply personal level. This connection enables CHWs to address health disparities and provide care that goes beyond medical treatments.

Titles/Role CHW

The roles and responsibilities of CHWs in Florida's health care systems vary greatly from outreach to health educator to screener to care coordinator to research team member. The exact mix of these roles and tasks for any one individual varies based on the needs of those served and the provider or organization for which the CHW is providing the service. There is lack of uniformity in the names/titles of CHWs across the health care delivery system.

Titles Community Health Workers are referred to as:

- Patient navigator
- Patient ambassador
- Community health aid
- Promotores de salud
- Coaches

- Lay health advisors
- Community health representatives
- Peer mentors
- Peer navigators

CHW Core Values

The foundation of community health workers rests on the core values that define their profession. These core values are based on the history, unique role, and ongoing development of the field. These core values reflect a broad definition of healthy communities and include:

- Access
- Acceptance
- Advocacy & education
- Excellence

- Learning
- Partnership
- Self-determination
- Social justice

- Strength
- Trust
- Unity

The National Association of Community Health Workers (NACHW) was founded in April 2019 after several years of planning and organizing by Community Health Workers (CHWs) and allies across the United States. NACHW is a 501(c)(3) nonprofit membership-driven organization with a mission to unify CHWs across geography, ethnicity, sector and experience to support communities to achieve health, equity and social justice.

Community Health Worker is an umbrella term and includes community health representatives, promotors, peers and **other workforce members** who are **frontline public health professionals** that share life experience, trust, compassion, cultural and value alignment with the communities where they live and serve.

Our values – *self-determination and self-empowerment of our workforce; integrity of character; dignity and respect for every human being, social justice and equity to ensure fair treatment, access, opportunity and outcomes for all individuals and communities* – guide our work. They are north stars we will use to support our members, foster partnerships, advocate nationally, develop strategic objectives, and assess our impact.

NACHW is led by an **Executive Director** who is also a CHW and enjoys governance from a national **Board of Directors** of predominately CHWs and allies with decades of research and practice expertise in CHW training and workforce development, community organizing and engagement, intervention design, equity and social justice advocacy, research and policy leadership.

Communication

When it comes to communication a Community Health Worker should have skills to communicate effectively.

Skills will include:

Conflict Resolution

- Ability to avoid or resolve conflicts.
- Write clearly so other people can understand
- Ability to prepare written communication (examples: client encounter documentation) including electronic communication (e.g., email, telecommunication device for the deaf, interpreters)
- Cultural understanding of patients and others.
- Understanding and connecting in culturally diversity settings.
- Nonverbal communication: Including perceiving patients' cues and concerns.
- Understand basic principles of verbal and non-verbal communication
- Listen actively, communicate with empathy and gather information in a respectful manner
- Use language confidently and appropriately - Identify barriers to communication
- Give information to clients and groups concisely

- Speak and write in client's preferred language and at appropriate literacy level - Document activities and services and prepare written documentation
- Collect data and provide feedback to health and human services agencies, funding sources, and community-based organizations
- Gather information in a respectful manner
- Assist in interpreting and/or translating health information

CHW Capacity -Building Skills

- Identify problems and resources to encourage and help clients solve problems themselves
- Collaborate with local partnerships to improve services, network and build community connections
- Learn new and better ways of serving the community through formal and informal training
- Assess the strengths and needs of the community - Build leadership skills for yourself and others in the community
- Facilitate support groups - Organize with others in the community to address health issues or other needs/concerns

Teaching Ability and Skills

- Participate in organizing others, use existing resources, and current data to promote a cause

- Read and understand work-related materials.
- Understand written information.
- Identify and work with advocacy groups - Inform health and social service systems and carry out mandatory reporting requirements
- Stay abreast of structural and policy changes in the community and in health and social services systems
- Speak up for individuals or communities to overcome intimidation and other barriers
- Utilize coping strategies for managing stress and staying healthy
- When you teach; check how well one is learning or doing something after teaching

CHW Organizational Skills and Capability

- Plan and set individual and organization goals
- Plan and set up presentations, educational/training sessions, workshops, and other activities
- Effectively manage time and prioritize activities, yet stay flexible
- Maintain and contribute to a safe working environment - Gather, document, and report on activities within legal and organization guidelines

Interpersonal Skills

- Represent others, their needs, and needs of the community
- Be sensitive, honest, respectful, and empathetic
- Establish relationships, and assist in individual and group conflict resolution
- Understand basic principles of culture, cultural competency, and cultural humility
- Recognize and appropriately respond to the beliefs, values, cultures, and languages of the populations served
- Be aware of others' reactions and understand the possible causes
- Set personal and professional boundaries
- Provide informal counseling
- Use interviewing techniques (e.g. motivational interviewing)
- Solve problems by bringing others together to discuss differences
- Work as a team member - Act within ethical responsibilities as set forth in Rules regarding Training and Certification of CHWs
- Professional and Ethical Standards to maintain confidentiality of client information and act within the Health Insurance Portability and Accountability Act (HIPAA) requirements
- Model behavior change - Ability to network with others

CHW Provider Service Coordination Skills

- Identify and access resources and maintain a current resource inventory
- Help improve access to resources - Conduct outreach to encourage participation in health events
- Coordinate CHW activities with clinical and other community services
- Develop networks to address community needs
- Coordinate referrals, follow-up, track care and referral outcomes
- Help others navigate services and resources in health and human services systems
- Provide education, assessment and social support to clients and communities

Assessment

Conducting Needs Assessments

1. Define the Problem You're Hoping to Address

One common mistake is looking too narrowly at your organization when documenting needs. For example, some administrators know they need to address a knowledge gap because of new cancer screening guidelines. But they forget to consider if their in-person training staff is qualified to handle online discussions. They assume that uploading a PDF toolkit to a website will be enough for everyone. Looking at only one piece of the puzzle will solve exactly one piece.

Once you've defined the problem, look at it from all angles. Ask yourself:

- What's causing the problem?
- Who's affected by it?
- How are they affected?
- What do you need to do to address it?
- Has anyone done anything about it yet? If so, what happened?
- What resources do you have to do something about it? How can you use them?

2. Find Out What Your Employees Need to Learn.

Next in your needs assessment, define what your learners need to know to address the problem. Do they need cultural communication techniques? Do they lack health literacy skills? Does your state require anything for certification? If so, start there.
You may also have results-based needs, such as addressing a growing population with an influx of volunteer community liaisons. Looking at gaps in learning will help you identify how to address them.

Note: You can ask your students what they want to learn but proceed down this road with caution. Sometimes, they don't know what they need and lack the terminology to tell you or have very little experience with (or love of) online learning.

3. Determine Gaps in Your Infrastructure.

Once you've identified what your audience needs to learn, your needs assessment needs to include a section about the weaknesses you see in your infrastructure to make that happen. For example, you might need to hire a new fleet of trainers with skills in **online teaching strategies. Or, your grant has reporting requirements,** and you'll need evaluation tools to address them. You also can group stakeholders with your infrastructure because they will also have requirements you'll need to address, such as the ability to become self-supporting with your new courses.
Decide on The Best Technology for Your Needs.

Knowing what your needs are for learning and for your infrastructure will help greatly when you analyze what kind of technology will work best for your organization. Then you can begin to decide if you need self-paced learning, instructor-led online courses (and what those instructors need) or a blended-learning program. When you have a list of digital tools and features you need, you can measure them against providers and vendors that can help address those. |

4. Define A Strategy and Objectives to Successfully Complete It.

Remember that a needs assessment is just the beginning. Look at it as the launching point for a deep investigation into what it will take for your program to succeed. Jumping into something for the sake of it might seem like a fast solution. But you'll be glad you took the time to look deeply into your requirements before you begin building.

Your strategy must clearly define the problem you're working on solving, the training your CHWs need to complete, and the steps your organization needs to follow in order to achieve a successful program. Break down the project into milestones to keep everyone aligned and report on progress more easily.

See sample form for working with patients or members!!!

Patient Medical Record Stamp

Patient Name _____ DOB ___/___/___
Date of visit: ___/___/___   Time spent with patient: ____ minutes   If Group Visit, number in group _____

Type of Visit:
- ☐ Individual
- ☐ Individual prior to provider visit
- ☐ Group education with CHW*
- ☐ Group with provider or other member of team*
- ☐ By telephone
- ☐ With Interpreter

* Complete a form for each patient/participant

Interventions during this visit: (check all that apply)

Teaching
- ☐ Self-management goal setting
- ☐ Review of previous self-management goal
- ☐ General Diabetes Information
- ☐ Healthful eating information
- ☐ Exercise strategies
- ☐ Glucose testing strategies
- ☐ Medication adherence strategies
- ☐ Other not listed :
_____

Referrals
- ☐ Lab
- ☐ Eye exam
- ☐ Podiatry
- ☐ Dental
- ☐ Information on classes:
- ☐ Benefits coordinator
- ☐ Community exercise classes
- ☐ Dietician
- ☐ Mental Health

*type*_____
- ☐ Other:
_____

Self-management behaviors/Ask the patient:
On how many of the last seven days….   *Circle number of days*

Have you followed a healthful eating plan?	0	1	2	3	4	5	6	7
Did you do at least 30 minutes of physical activity? (including walking)	0	1	2	3	4	5	6	7
Did you test your blood sugar?	0	1	2	3	4	5	6	7
Did you check your feet?	0	1	2	3	4	5	6	7
Did you take your recommended diabetes medicine?	0	1	2	3	4	5	6	7

Which one of these statements comes closest to the patient's plans for managing his or her diabetes?/Ask the patient:
- ☐ I am not interested in managing my diabetes (Pre-contemplative)
- ☐ I know it is important for me to make changes to mange my diabetes, but I am not ready yet (Contemplative)
- ☐ I plan to make changes to manage my diabetes in the next few months (Preparation)
- ☐ I am ready to make changes to manage my diabetes (Action)
- ☐ I have been able to meet and continue to meet the goal I have set to manage my diabetes (Maintenance)
- ☐ I have returned to my previous behaviors (Relapse)

Identified Self-Management Goal:
What?	
When?	
Where?	
How often?	

How confident is your patient that he or she can achieve the identified goal:
☐ Very confident ☐ Somewhat confident ☐ Neither confident or unsure ☐ Somewhat unsure ☐ Very unsure

Patient ID #:	CHC:	CHW:

5. Define Your Performance Measures.

Before implementing any online training program, you'll need to define the key performance indicators that will tell you whether the initiative is successful or not. Some metrics you could consider include certifications achieved or completion rates. But you'll have to evaluate internally what your goal is based on the program's objectives and the problem you're addressing.

6. Set A Budget.

Finally, once you've defined exactly what the program needs to look like to solve the problem, it's time to set a realistic budget. It may seem counterintuitive to list this step at the end, but entering the needs assessment with a budget in mind may hinder your ability to take all factors into account — after all, if you're focusing on a number from the beginning, you may have a skewed perception of what your organization needs or how it can achieve it within that constraint. Plus, it's hard to set a budget without a clear view of what your program needs in the first place.

Cultural Responsiveness

Culture is defined here as beliefs, values, customs, and social behavior shared by a group of people with common identity. The CHWs act as cultural mediators by:

Improving services and reducing disparities. Identity may be based on race, ethnicity, language, religion, sex, gender identity, sexual orientation, disability, health condition, education, income, place, profession, history, or other factors.

Culture also includes organizational cultures, which are reflected in how organizations deliver services. The CHWs encourage and help enable individuals to participate in decisions that affect their lives, families, and communities.

Competency includes the ability to:

Recognize different aspects of community and culture and how these can influence peoples' health beliefs and behavior.

Recognize ways the organizational culture within provider agencies and institutions can affect access, quality, and individual experience with services.

Employ techniques for interacting sensitively and effectively with people from cultures or communities that differ from one's own.

Support the development of authentic, effective partnerships between individuals and providers by helping each to better understand the other's perspectives.

Implement accommodations to address communication needs accurately and sensitively with people whose language(s) one cannot understand.

Advocate for and promote the use of culturally and linguistically appropriate services and resources within organizations and with diverse colleagues and community partners.

Initiate and sustain trusting relationships with individuals, families, and social networks.

Adult Learning

What Are Adult Learning Principles?

There are 10 simple principles of adult learning for future educators to keep in mind. All of these aspects are important when building curriculum and expectations for adult learners:

1. Adults Are Self-Directing: For many adults, self-directed learning happens naturally without anyone explaining it or suggesting it. Adult learners are more prone to plan, carry out, and evaluate their learning experiences without the help of others. When instructing adults, it's important for learners to set goals, determine their educational or training needs, and implement a plan to enhance their own learning.

2. Adults Learn by Doing: Many adults prefer not only to read or hear about subjects but to actively participate in projects and to take actions related to their learning. Project-based curriculum utilizes real-world scenarios and creates projects for students that they could encounter in a job in the future. Many adult learners find that this kind of learning is hugely beneficial for them as they apply what they have been taught to their careers, giving them direct access to seeing what they can do with their knowledge.

3. Adults Desire Relevance: While some enjoy learning as an end in itself, adult learners are more likely to engage in learning that has direct relevance to their lives. For example, if they're taking a certification course to improve their chances of promotion on the job, then the course should immediately address their needs.

4. Adults Utilize Experience: Adults are shaped by their experiences, and the best learning comes from making sense of those experiences. Adult learners can greatly benefit from finding ways to get hands-on learning. Internships, job shadowing opportunities, projects, and other experiential opportunities can help them get a firmer grasp of their learning and be more excited about how what they learn can be applied to their interests and careers.

5. Adults Process with Their Senses: Most adult learners don't thrive as well in a lecture-style environment. Due to the lack of brain plasticity in older learners, it's important to fully engage the senses when learning to successfully solidify new knowledge. Learning practices need to incorporate audio, visual, reading/writing, kinesthetic, independent, and group techniques.

6. Adults Appreciate Repetition: Repetition is essential for adult learning. If learners can practice new skills in a supportive environment, self-efficacy will develop to take those skills outside of the classroom. And the more they can practice a particular subject or skill, the better the chances are for mastery.

7. Adults Guide Their Own Development: Utilizing dilemmas and situations to challenge an adult learner's assumptions and principles helps them guide their own development. Adults can use critical thinking and questioning to evaluate their underlying beliefs and assumptions and learn from what they realize about themselves in the process.

8. Adults Thrive with Goal Setting: Learners who have a specific career or personal goal in mind will have a better experience as they pursue their degree programs. For example, if a student wants to learn Spanish before a trip to Mexico, they might have a specific goal to be conversational by a certain date. Adult learners need these goals because their learning is more in their own hands than younger learners.

9. Adults Learn Differently Than Children: Children and adults are very different when it comes to how they learn, so different techniques must be used in order to make learning effective for adults. In addition to reading and memorizing, adult learners utilize their past life experiences and their current understanding of a subject as they learn. Also, adult learning needs to be problem-centered, making the impact more focused on current events or real life.

10. Adults Require Ownership: With a more nuanced and advanced hierarchy of needs, adult learners place more value on intrinsic motivation and personal ownership of their learning. It's important to give adults internal motivation by recognizing their success and promoting increased self-esteem and confidence.

CHW Code of Ethics

- Ability to set goals and to develop and observe a work plan
- Ability to balance priorities and to manage time
- Ability to apply critical thinking techniques, problem solving, and identify when follow-up is needed with the appropriate multi-disciplinary teams
- Ability to use pertinent technology
- Ability to observe and follow ethical and legal standards (e.g. CHW Code of Ethics, Americans with Disabilities Act [ADA], Health Insurance Portability and Accountability Act [HIPAA])
- Ability to identify situations calling for mandatory reporting and carry out mandatory reporting requirements

- Ability to participate in professional development of peer CHWs and in networking among CHW groups
- Ability to set boundaries and practice self-care

The American Association of Community Health Workers Code of Ethics

A Community Health Worker (CHW) is a frontline public health worker who is a trusted member of and/or has an unusually close understating of the community she or he serves.

This trusting relationship enables the CHW to serve as a liaison/link/intermediary between health/social services and the community to facilitate access to services and improve the quality and cultural competence of service delivery. A CHW also builds individual and community capacity by increasing health knowledge and self-sufficiency through a range of activities such as outreach, community edge and self-sufficiency through a range of activities such as outreach, community education, informal counseling, social support, and advocacy.

Purpose of This Code

The CHW Code of Ethics is bases on and supported by the core values adopted by the American Association of SHWs. The Code of Ethics outlines in this document provides a framework for SHWs, Supervisors, and employers of CHWs to discuss ethical issues facing the profession. Employers are encouraged to consider this Code when creating CHW programs. The responsibility of all CHWs is to strive for excellence by providing quality service and the most accurate information available to individuals, families, and communities.

The Code of Ethics is based upon commonly understood principles that apply to all professionals within the health and social service fields (e.g., promotion of social justice, positive health, and dignity). The Code, however, does not address all ethical issues facing CHWs and the absence of a rule does not imply that there is no ethical obligation present. As professionals, CHWs are encouraged to reflect on the ethical obligations that they have to the communities that they serve, and to share these reflections with others.

Article 1. Responsibility in the Delivery of Care

CHWs build trust and community capacity by improving the health and social welfare of the client they serve. When a conflict arises among individuals, groups, agencies, or institutions, CHWs should consider all issues and give priority to those that promote the wellness and quality of living for the individual/client. The following provisions promote the professional integrity of CHWs.

1.1 Honesty CHWs are professionals that strive to ensure the best health outcomes for the communities they serve. They communicate the potential benefits and consequences of available services, including the programs they are employed under.

1.2 Confidentiality CHWs respect the confidentiality, privacy, and trust of individuals, families, and communities that they serve. They understand and abide by employer policies, as well as state and federal confidentiality laws that are relevant to their work.

1.3 Scope of Ability and Training CHWs are truthful about qualifications, competencies, and limitations on services they may provide, and should not misrepresent qualifications or competencies to individuals, families, communities or employers.

1.4 Quality of Care CHWs strive to provide high quality services to individuals, families, and communities. They do this through continued education, training, and an obligation to ensure the information they provide is up-to-date and accurate.

1.5 Referral of Appropriate Services CHWs acknowledge when client issues are outside of their scope of practice and refer clients to the appropriate health, wellness, or social support services when necessary.

1.6 Legal Obligations CHWs have an obligation to report actual or potential harm to individuals within the communities they serve to the appropriate authorities. CHWs have a responsibility to follow requirements set by states, the federal government, and/or their employing organizations. Responsibility of the larger society or specific legal obligations may supersede the loyalty owed to individual community members.

Article 2. Promotion of Equitable Relationships

CHWs focus their efforts on the well-being of the whole community. They value and respect the expertise and knowledge that each community member possesses. IN turn, CHWs strive to create equitable partnerships with communities to address all issues of health and well-being.

2.1 Cultural Humility SHWs possess expertise in the communities in which they serve. They maintain a high degree of humility and respect for the cultural diversity within each community. As advocates for their communities, CHWs have an obligation to inform employers and others when policies and procedures will offend or harm communities or are ineffective within the communities where they work.

2.2 Maintaining the Trust of the Community CHWs are often members of their communities and their effectiveness in providing services derived from the trust placed in them by member of these communities. CHWs do not act in ways that could jeopardize the trust placed in them by the communities they serve.

2.3 Respect for Human Rights CHWs maintain professional relationships with clients. They establish, respect, and actively maintain personal boundaries between them and their clients.

2.4 Anti-Discrimination CHWs do not discriminate against any person or group on the basis of race, ethnicity, gender, sexual orientation, age, religion, social status, disability, or immigration status.

2.5 Client Relationship CHWs maintain professional relationships with clients. They establish, respect, and actively maintain personal boundaries between them and their clients

Article 3. Interactions with Other Service Providers

3.1 Cooperation CHWs place the well-being of those they serve above personal disagreements and work cooperatively with any other person or organization dedicated to providing care to those in need.

3.2 Conduct CHWs promote integrity in the delivery of health and social services. They respect the rights, dignity, and worth of all people and have an ethical obligation to report any inappropriate behavior (e.g., sexual harassment, racial discrimination, etc.) to the proper authority.

3.3 Self-Presentation CHWs are truthful and forthright in presenting their background and training to other service providers.

Article 4. Professional Rights and Responsibilities

The CHW profession is dedicated to excellence in the practice of promoting well-being in communities. Guided by common values, CHWs have the responsibility to uphold the principles and integrity of the profession as they assist families to make decisions impacting their wellbeing. CHWs embrace the individual, family, and community strengths and build upon them to increase community capacity.

4.1 Continuing Education CHWs should remain up to date on any developments that substantially affect their ability to competently render services. CHWs strive to expand their professional knowledge base and competencies through education and participation in professional organizations.

4.2 Advocacy for Chance in Law and Policy CHWs are advocates for change and work on impacting policies that promote social justice and hold systems accountable for being responsive to communities.

4.3 Enhancing Community Capacity CHWs assist individuals and communities in moving towards self-sufficiency in order to promote the creation of opportunities and resources that support their autonomy

4.4 Wellness and Safety CHWs are sensitive to their own personal well-being (physical, mental, and spiritual health) and strive to maintain a safe environment for themselves and the communities they serve.

4.5 Loyalty to the Profession CHWs are advocates for the profession. They are members, leaders, and active participants in the local, state, and national professional organizations.

4.6 Advocacy for the Profession CHWs are advocates for the profession. They are members, leaders, and active participants in local, state, and national professional organizations.

4.7 Recognition of Others CHWs give recognition to others for their professional contributions and achievements.

Documentation

CHWs help promote coordinated and effective services by documenting their work activities by:

- Writing summaries of individual and community assessments accurately
- Present information to organizational colleagues or community partners about the individuals and issues they face while respecting peoples' privacy.

Competency includes the ability to:

- Reflect, organize and write in a way that communicates effectively with individuals, other community members, supervisors, and other professional colleagues.
- Comply with reporting, record keeping, and documentation requirements in one's work.
- Use appropriate technology, such as computers, for work-based communication, according to employer requirements.
- Recognize the importance of timely and accurate documentation to program evaluation, sustainability and to help individuals achieve their goals.

OSHA

With the Occupational Safety and Health Act of 1970, Congress created the Occupational Safety and Health Administration (OSHA) to ensure safe and healthful working conditions for workers by setting and enforcing standards and by providing training, outreach, education and assistance.

The **Occupational Safety and Health (OSH) Act** was enacted to "assure safe and healthful working conditions for working men and women." The OSH Act created the **Occupational Safety and Health Administration (OSHA)** at the federal level and provided that states could run their own safety and health programs as long as those programs were at least as effective as the federal program. Federal and state safety personnel work to ensure worker safety and health through work site enforcement, education and compliance assistance, and cooperative and voluntary programs. Enforcement and administration of the OSH Act in states under federal jurisdiction is handled primarily by OSHA. Safety and health standards related to field sanitation and certain temporary labor camps in the agriculture industry are enforced by the U.S. Department of Labor's <u>Wage and Hour Division (WHD)</u> in states under federal jurisdiction. If a work site is located in a <u>state plan state</u>, additional safety and health requirements may apply.

ADA

Introduction to the Americans with Disabilities Act

The Americans with Disabilities Act (ADA) is a federal civil rights law that prohibits discrimination against people with disabilities in everyday activities. The ADA prohibits discrimination based on disability just as other civil rights laws prohibit discrimination on the basis of race, color, sex, national origin, age, and religion. The ADA guarantees that people with disabilities have the same opportunities as everyone else to enjoy employment opportunities, purchase goods and services, and participate in state and local government programs.

The ADA Protects People with Disabilities

A person with a disability is someone who:

- has a physical or mental impairment that substantially limits one or more major life activities,
- has a history or record of such an impairment (such as cancer that is in remission), or
- is perceived by others as having such an impairment (such as a person who has scars from a severe burn).

If a person falls into any of these categories, the ADA protects them. Because the ADA is a law, and not a benefit program, you do not need to apply for coverage.

What do *substantial limits* mean?

The term "substantially limits" is interpreted broadly and is not meant to be a demanding standard. But not every condition will meet this standard. An example of a condition that is not substantially limiting is a mild allergy to pollen.

What do *major life activities* mean?

Major life activities are the kind of activities that you do every day, including your body's own internal processes. There are many major life activities in addition to the examples listed here. Some examples include:

- Actions like eating, sleeping, speaking, and breathing
- Movements like walking, standing, lifting, and bending

- Cognitive functions like thinking and concentrating
- Sensory functions like seeing and hearing
- Tasks like working, reading, learning, and communicating
- The operation of major bodily functions like circulation, reproduction, and individual organs

Examples of Disabilities

There is a wide variety of disabilities, and the ADA regulations do not list all of them. Some disabilities are visible, and some are not. Some examples of disabilities include:

- Cancer
- Diabetes
- Post-traumatic stress disorder
- HIV
- Autism
- Cerebral palsy
- Deafness or hearing loss
- Blindness or low vision
- Epilepsy
- Mobility disabilities such as those requiring the use of a wheelchair, walker, or cane
- Intellectual disabilities
- Major depressive disorder
- Traumatic brain injury

The ADA covers many other disabilities not listed here.

The ADA Prohibits Disability Discrimination in Many Areas of Life

To prevent discrimination against people with disabilities, the ADA sets out requirements that apply to many of the situations you encounter in everyday life. Employers, state and local governments, businesses that are open to the public, commercial facilities, transportation providers, and telecommunication companies all have to follow the requirements of the ADA.

The ADA prohibits discrimination based on disability.

The ADA is broken up into five different sections, which are called titles. Different titles set out the requirements for different kinds of organizations. For example, Title I of the ADA covers requirements for employers, and Title II covers requirements for state and local governments. You can find the relevant title of the ADA noted next to each type of organization below.

Employment

Section of the ADA: Title I

Applies to employers that have 15 or more employees, including state/local governments, employment agencies, and labor unions.

General requirement: Employers must provide people with disabilities an equal opportunity to benefit from the employment-related opportunities available to others. This includes things like recruitment, hiring, promotions, training, pay, and social activities.

The ADA includes specific requirements for employers to ensure that people with disabilities have equal access to employment. Learn more about these requirements on the **Equal Employment Opportunity Commission's guidance for employers.**

How to file a complaint: File a Charge of Discrimination with the Equal Employment Opportunity Commission.

State and Local Government

Section of the ADA: Title II, Subtitle A

Applies to all services, programs, and activities of state and local governments.

Examples of state and local government activities include:

- Public education
- Transportation
- Recreation
- Health care
- Social services
- Courts
- Voting
- Emergency services
- Town meetings

The ADA applies to state and local governments even if:

- the state or local government is small or
- They receive money from the federal government.

General requirement: State and local governments must provide people with disabilities an equal opportunity to benefit from all of their programs, services, and activities.

The ADA contains specific requirements for state and local governments to ensure equal access for people with disabilities. Learn about these requirements in the **State and Local Government Primer.**

How to file a complaint: File a complaint with the U.S. Department of Justice.

Public Transit

Section of the ADA: Title II, Subtitle B

Applies to public transit systems.

General requirement: Public transit systems must provide people with disabilities an equal opportunity to benefit from their services.

Note: Private transit systems are also covered by the ADA. For more information, see the section **Businesses that are open to the public** below.

Businesses Open to The Public

Section of the ADA: Title III

Applies to:

- Businesses and nonprofits serving the public. Examples of businesses and nonprofits include:
  - Restaurants
  - Hotels
  - Retail stores
  - Movie theaters
  - Private schools (including housing)
  - Doctors' offices and hospitals
  - Day care centers
  - Gyms
  - Organizations offering courses or examinations
- Privately operated transit. Examples of privately operated transit include:
  - Taxis
  - Intercity and charter buses
  - Hotel shuttles
  - Airport shuttles
- Commercial facilities need only comply with the requirements of the **ADA Standards for Accessible Design.** Examples of commercial facilities include:

- o Office buildings
- o Warehouses
- o Factories

General requirement: Businesses must provide people with disabilities an equal opportunity to access the goods or services that they offer.

The ADA contains specific requirements for businesses that are open to the public. Learn more about these requirements: **ADA Primer for Small Businesses**.

How to file a complaint: File a complaint with the U.S. Department of Justice.

Telecommunications

Section of the ADA: Title IV

Applies to telecommunication companies.

General requirement: Telephone companies must provide services to allow callers with hearing and speech disabilities to communicate.

How to file a complaint: Contact the Telecommunications Relay Services point of contact for your state through the Federal Communications Commission.

Other Important Requirements

Section of the ADA: Title V

The ADA also includes other requirements for how to implement the law. Examples of these requirements include:

- Prohibiting retaliation against a person who has asserted their rights under the ADA
- Stating that a person with a disability is not required to accept an aid or accommodation if they do not want to
- Authorizing courts to award attorneys' fees to the winning party in a lawsuit under the ADA
- Directing certain federal agencies to issue guidance explaining the law

Other Disability Rights Laws

Although the ADA applies to many areas of life, it does not cover everything. In some situations, disability discrimination is prohibited by laws other than the ADA.

While the ADA applies to certain types of housing (e.g., housing at private and public universities and public housing programs), the Fair Housing Act applies to many types of housing, both public and privately owned, including housing covered by the ADA.

- If you have a complaint about disability discrimination under the Fair Housing Act: **File a complaint with the Department of Housing and Urban Development**.

Disability discrimination during air travel is prohibited by the Air Carriers Access Act.

- If you have a complaint about disability discrimination during air travel: **File a complaint with the Department of Transportation's Office of Aviation Consumer Protection.**

Religious organizations are exempt from the requirements of Title III of the ADA. For information about how the ADA's employment obligations apply to religious entities, visit the EEOC's website. Additionally, religious groups or organizations may still have to comply with state/local building codes or other laws prohibiting discrimination on the basis of disability.

Federal Agencies' Roles

Many federal agencies are responsible for enforcing the ADA and other laws that prohibit discrimination on the basis of disability. These agencies receive complaints, conduct investigations, and issue regulations and guidance to explain the law.

Learn more about these agencies and the laws that they implement:

- **ADA Designated Investigative Services**
- **A Guide to Federal Disability Rights Laws**

HIPAA

Health Insurance Portability & Accountability Act

The Health Insurance Portability and Accountability Act (HIPAA) Privacy, Security, and Breach Notification Rules protect the privacy and security of health information and give patients' rights to their health information. HIPAA establishes standards to safeguard the protected health information (PHI) that you hold if you're one of these covered entities or their business associate:

- Health plan

- Health care clearinghouse

- Health care provider that conducts certain health care transactions electronically

Privacy Rule

The Privacy Rule protects your patients' PHI while letting you securely exchange information to coordinate your patients' care. The Privacy Rule also gives patients the right to:

- Examine and get a copy of their medical records, including an electronic copy of their medical records
- Request corrections
- Restrict their health plan's access to information about treatments they paid for in cash

Under the Privacy Rule, most health plans can't use or disclose genetic information for underwriting purposes. You're allowed to report child abuse or neglect to the authorities.

PHI

The Privacy Rule protects PHI that you hold or transmit in any form, including electronic, paper, or verbal. PHI includes information about:

- Common identifiers, such as name, address, birth date, and SSN
- The patient's past, present, or future physical or mental health condition
- Health care you provide to the patient
- The past, present, or future payment for health care you provide to the patient

Requirements

The Privacy Rule requires you to:

- Notify patients about their privacy rights and how you use their information
- Adopt privacy procedures and train employees to follow them
- Assign an individual to make sure you're adopting and following privacy procedures
- Secure patient records containing PHI, so they aren't readily available to those who don't need to see them

Sharing Information with Other Health Care Professionals

To coordinate your patient's care with other providers, the Privacy Rule lets you:

- Share information with doctors, hospitals, and ambulances for treatment, payment, and health care operations, even without a signed consent form from the patient
- Share information about an incapacitated patient if you believe it's in your patient's best interest
- Use health information for research purposes

- Use email, phone, or fax machines to communicate with other health care professionals and with patients, if you use safeguards

Sharing Patient Information with Family Members & Others

Unless a patient objects, the Privacy Rule lets you:

- Give information to a patient's family, friends, or anyone else the patient identifies as involved in their care
- Give information about the patient's general condition or location to a patient's family member or anyone responsible for the patient's care
- Include basic information in a hospital directory, such as the patient's phone and room number
- Give information about a patient's religious affiliation to clergy members

Incidental Disclosures

The HIPAA Privacy Rule requires you to have policies that protect and limit how you use and disclose PHI, but you aren't expected to guarantee the privacy of PHI against all risks. Sometimes, you can't reasonably prevent limited disclosures, even when you're following HIPAA requirements.

For example, a hospital visitor may overhear a doctor's confidential conversation with a nurse or glimpse a patient's information on a sign-in sheet. These incidental disclosures aren't a HIPAA violation as long as you're following the required reasonable safeguards.

The Office for Civil Rights (OCR) offers guidance about how this applies to health care practices, including incidental uses and disclosures FAQs.

Visit HHS HIPAA Guidance Materials for information about:

- De-identifying PHI to meet HIPAA Privacy Rule requirements

- Patients' right to access health information

- Permitted uses and disclosures of PHI

Security Rule

- The Security Rule includes security requirements to protect patients' electronic PHI (ePHI) confidentiality, integrity, and availability. The Security Rule requires you to:
- Develop reasonable and appropriate security policies
- Ensure the confidentiality, integrity, and availability of all ePHI you create, get, maintain, or transmit
- Identify and protect against threats to ePHI security or integrity

- Protect against impermissible uses or disclosures
- Analyze security risks in your environment and create appropriate solutions
- Review and modify security measures to continue protecting ePHI in a changing environment
- Ensure employee compliance

When developing compliant safety measures, consider:

- Size, complexity, and capabilities
- Technical, hardware, and software infrastructure
- The costs of security measures
- The likelihood and possible impact of risks to ePHI

Visit HHS Cyber Security Guidance Material for information about:

- Administrative, physical, and technical PHI safety measures
- Cybersecurity
- Remote and mobile use of ePHI

Breach Notification Rule

When you experience a PHI breach, the Breach Notification Rule requires you to notify affected patients, HHS, and, in some cases, the media. Generally, a breach is an unpermitted use or disclosure under the Privacy Rule that compromises the security or privacy of PHI. The unpermitted use or disclosure of PHI is a breach unless there's a low probability the PHI has been compromised, based on a risk assessment of:

- The nature and extent of the PHI involved, including types of identifiers and the likelihood of re-identification
- The unauthorized person who used the PHI or got the disclosed PHI
- Whether an individual acquired or viewed the PHI
- The extent to which you reduced the PHI risk

You must notify authorities of most breaches without reasonable delay and no later than 60 days after discovering the breach. Submit notifications of smaller breaches affecting fewer than 500 patients to HHS annually. The Breach Notification Rule also requires your business associates to notify you of breaches at or by the business associate.

Visit the HHS Breach Notification Rule for information about:

- Administrative requirements and burden of proof
- How to make unsecured PHI unusable, unreadable, or indecipherable to unauthorized individuals
- Reporting requirements

Who Must Comply with HIPAA Rules?

Covered entities and business associates must follow HIPAA rules. If you don't meet the definition of a covered entity or business associate, you don't have to comply with the HIPAA rules.

Learn more about covered entities and business associates, including fast facts for covered entities.

For definitions of covered entities and business associates, see 45 CFR 160.103.

Who Enforces HIPAA Rules?

The HHS OCR enforces the HIPAA Privacy, Security, and Breach Notification Rules. Violations may result in civil monetary penalties. In some cases, U.S. Department of Justice enforced criminal penalties may apply. Common violations include:

- Unpermitted PHI use and disclosure
- Use or disclosure of more than the minimum necessary PHI
- Lack of PHI safeguards
- Lack of administrative, technical, or physical ePHI safeguards
- Lack of patients' access to their PHI

Medicare PART A, B, C, D

Parts of Medicare

There are different parts of Medicare to match your medical coverage needs and budget.

Parts A and B

You'll sign up for Medicare through Social Security. You can sign up for Parts A and B, or Part A only.

Part A (hospital insurance)

Part A helps pay for inpatient care at:

- Hospitals
- Skilled nursing facilities
- Hospice

It also covers some outpatient home health.

Part A is free if you worked and paid Medicare taxes for at least 10 years. You may also be eligible because of your current or former spouse's work.

Part B (medical insurance)

Part B helps cover:

- Services from doctors and other health care providers
- Outpatient care
- Home health care
- Durable medical equipment
- Some preventive services

Most people pay a monthly premium for Part B. The exact premium depends on your income level. Review what you might pay for Medicare at Medicare.gov.

Parts C and D

Private companies run Parts C and D. The federal government approves each plan. Costs and coverage types vary by provider.

Part C (Medicare Advantage)

Part C is known as Medicare Advantage. It's an alternative to Parts A and B that bundles several coverage types, including Parts A, B, and usually D. It may also include:

- Vision
- Hearing
- Dental insurance

You must sign up for Part A or Part B before enrolling in a Medicare Advantage plan.

Part D (prescription drug coverage)

Part D helps cover prescription drug costs.

You must sign up for Part A or Part B before enrolling in Part D.

Get started with Parts C and D

Review and sign up for Medicare Advantage and drug plans on Medicare.gov.

33

Social Determinants

Community Health Workers (CHW) Knowledge - Specific Health Issues

- Gain and share basic knowledge of the community, health and social services, specific health issues
- Understand social determinants of health and health disparities - Stay current on health issues affecting clients and know where to find answers to difficult questions
- Understand consumer rights - Find information on specific health topics and issues across all ages [lifespan focus], including healthy lifestyles, maternal and child health, heart disease & stroke, diabetes, cancer, oral health and behavioral health
- Use and apply public health concepts as it relates to providing support and help to resources.

What is Health Equity?

Health Equity exists when all people, regardless of race, sex, sexual orientation, disability, socio-economic status, geographic location, or other societal constructs have fair and just access, opportunity, and resources to achieve their highest potential for health.

Unfortunately, social and political determinants of health negatively affect many communities, their people, and their ability to lead healthy lives.

Social Determinants of Health

What are the social determinants of health?   Social determinants of health (SDOH) are the conditions in the environments where people are born, live, work, play, worship, and age that affect a wide range of health, functioning, and quality of life outcomes and risks.

SDOH can be grouped into **five** domains:

- Economic Stability
- Education Access and Quality
- Healthcare Access and Quality
- Neighborhood and Built Environment
- Social and Community Context

Social determinants of health (SDOH) have a major impact on people's health, well-being, and quality of life. Examples of SDOH include:

- Safe housing, transportation, and neighborhoods
- Racism, discrimination, and violence

- Education, job opportunities, and income
- Access to nutritious foods and physical activity opportunities
- Polluted air and water
- Language and literacy skills

SDOH also contributes to wide health disparities and inequities. For example, people who don't have access to grocery stores with healthy foods are less likely to have good nutrition. That raises their risk of health conditions like heart disease, diabetes, and obesity — and even lowers life expectancy relative to people who do have access to healthy foods.

Just promoting healthy choices won't eliminate these and other health disparities. Instead, public health organizations and their partners in sectors like education, transportation, and housing need to take action to improve the conditions in people's environments.

WHO describes Social Determinants?

The social determinants of health (SDH) are the non-medical factors that influence health outcomes. They are the conditions in which people are born, grow, work, live, and age, and the wider set of forces and systems shaping the conditions of daily life. These forces and systems include economic policies and systems, development agendas, social norms, social policies and political systems.

The SDH has an important influence on health inequities - the unfair and avoidable differences in health status seen within and between countries. In countries at all levels of income, health and illness follow a social gradient: the lower the socioeconomic position, the worse the health.

The following list provides examples of the social determinants of health, which can influence health equity in positive and negative ways:

- Income and social protection
- Education
- Unemployment and job insecurity
- Working life conditions
- Food insecurity
- Housing, basic amenities and the environment
- Early childhood development
- Social inclusion and non-discrimination
- Structural conflict
- Access to affordable health services of decent quality.

Research shows that social determinants can be more important than health care or lifestyle choices in influencing health. For example, numerous studies suggest that SDH accounts for between 30-55% of health outcomes. In addition, estimates show that the contribution of sectors outside health to population health outcomes exceeds the contribution from the health sector.

Addressing SDH appropriately is fundamental for improving health and reducing longstanding inequities in health, which requires action by all sectors and civil society.

Health Policy of Georgetown University

Cultural Competence in Health Care: Is it important for people with chronic conditions?

The increasing diversity of the nation brings opportunities and challenges for health care providers, health care systems, and policy makers to create and deliver culturally competent services. Cultural competence is defined as the ability of providers and organizations to effectively deliver health care services that meet the social, cultural, and linguistic needs of patients. A culturally competent health care system can help improve health outcomes and quality of care and can contribute to the elimination of racial and ethnic health disparities. Examples of strategies to move the health care system towards these goals include providing relevant training on cultural competence and cross-cultural issues to health professionals and creating policies that reduce administrative and linguistic barriers to patient care.

Racial and ethnic minorities are disproportionately burdened by chronic illness

Racial and ethnic minorities have higher morbidity and mortality from chronic diseases. The consequences can range from greater financial burden to higher activity limitations.

Among older adults, a higher proportion of African Americans and Latinos, compared to Whites, report that they have at least one of seven chronic conditions — asthma, cancer, heart disease, diabetes, high blood pressure, obesity, or anxiety/ depression. These rank among the costliest medical conditions in America.

African Americans and American Indians/Alaska Natives are more likely to be limited in an activity (e.g., work, walking, bathing, or dressing) due to chronic conditions.

The population at risk for chronic conditions will become more diverse

Although chronic illnesses or disabilities may occur at any age, the likelihood that a person will experience any activity limitation due to a chronic condition increases with age.(5) In 2000, 35 million people — more than 12 percent of the total population — were 65 years or older.(6) By 2050, it is expected that one in five Americans — 20 percent — will be elderly. The population will also become increasingly diverse (see Figure 2). By 2050, racial and ethnic minorities will comprise 35 percent of the over 65 population. (7) As the population at risk of chronic conditions becomes increasingly diverse, more attention to linguistic and cultural barriers to care will be necessary.

Access to health care differs by race and ethnicity

Having a regular doctor or a usual source of care facilitates the process of obtaining health care when it is needed. People who do not have a regular doctor or health care provider are less likely to obtain preventive services, or diagnosis, treatment, and management of chronic conditions. Health insurance coverage is also an important determinant of access to health care. Higher proportions of minorities compared to Whites do not have a usual source of care and do not have health insurance

Language and communication barriers are problematic

Of the more than 37 million adults in the U.S. who speak a language other than English, some 18 million people — 48 percent — report that they speak English less than "very well." (Language and communication barriers can affect the amount and quality of health care received. For example, Spanish-speaking Latinos are less likely than Whites to visit a physician or mental health provider, or receive preventive care, such as a mammography exam or influenza vaccination. Health service use may also be affected by the availability of interpreters. Among non-English speakers who needed an interpreter during a health care visit, less than half — 48 percent — report that they always or usually had one.

Language and communication problems may also lead to patient dissatisfaction, poor comprehension and adherence, and lower quality of care. Spanish-speaking Latinos are less satisfied with the care they receive and more likely to report overall problems with health care than are English speakers. The type of interpretation service provided to patients is an important factor in the level of satisfaction. In a study comparing various methods of interpretation, patients who use professional interpreters are equally as satisfied with the overall health care visit as patients who use bilingual providers. Patients who use family interpreters or non-professional interpreters, such as nurses, clerks, and technicians are less satisfied with their visit.

Low literacy also affects access to health care

The 1992 National Adult Literacy Survey found that 40 to 44 million Americans do not have the necessary literacy skills for daily functioning. The elderly typically have lower levels of literacy and have had less access to formal education than younger populations. Older patients with chronic diseases may need to make multiple and complex decisions about the management of their conditions. Racial and ethnic minorities are also more likely to have lower levels of literacy, often due to cultural and language barriers and differing educational opportunities. Low literacy may affect patients' ability to read and understand instructions on prescription or medicine bottles, health educational materials, and insurance forms, for example. Those with low literacy skills use more health services, and the resulting costs are estimated to be $32 to $58 billion — 3 to 6 percent — in additional health care expenditures.

Lack of cultural competence may lead to patient dissatisfaction

People with chronic conditions require more health services, therefore increasing their interaction with the health care system. If the providers, organizations, and systems are not working together to provide culturally competent care, patients are at higher risk of having negative health consequences, receiving poor quality care, or being dissatisfied with their care. African Americans and other ethnic minorities report less partnership with physicians, less participation in medical decisions, and lower levels of satisfaction with care. The quality of patient-physician interactions is lower among non-White patients, particularly Latinos and Asian Americans. Lower quality patient-physician interactions are associated with lower overall satisfaction with health care.

African Americans, Latinos, and Asian Americans are more likely than Whites to report that they believe they would have received better care if they had been of a different race or ethnicity. African Americans are more likely than other minority groups to feel that they were treated disrespectfully during a health care visit (e.g., they were spoken to rudely, talked down to, or ignored). Compared to other minority groups, Asian Americans are least likely to feel that their doctor understood their background and values and are most likely to report that their doctor looked down on them.

WHAT IS CULTURAL COMPETENCE IN HEALTH CARE?

Individual values, beliefs, and behaviors about health and well-being are shaped by various factors such as race, ethnicity, nationality, language, gender, socioeconomic status, physical and mental ability, sexual orientation, and occupation. Cultural competence in health care is broadly defined as the ability of providers and organizations to understand and integrate these factors into the delivery and structure of the health care system. The goal of culturally competent health care services is to provide the highest quality of care to every patient, regardless of race, ethnicity, cultural background, English proficiency or literacy. Some common strategies for improving the patient-provider interaction and institutionalizing changes in the health care system include:

1. Provide interpreter services

2. Recruit and retain minority staff

3. Provide training to increase cultural awareness, knowledge, and skills

4. Coordinate with traditional healers

5. Use community health workers

6. Incorporate culture-specific attitudes and values into health promotion tools

7. Include family and community members in health care decision making

8. Locate clinics in geographic areas that are easily accessible for certain populations

9. Expand hours of operation

10. Provide linguistic competency that extends beyond the clinical encounter to the appointment desk, advice lines, medical billing, and other written materials

Cultural competence is an ongoing learning process

In order to increase the cultural competence of the health care delivery system, health professionals must be taught how to provide services in a culturally competent manner. Although many different types of training courses have been developed across the country, these efforts have not been standardized or incorporated into training for health profession- also in any consistent manner.(21) Training courses vary greatly in content and teaching method, and may range from three-hour seminars to semester-long academic courses. Important to note, however, is that cultural competence is a process rather than an ultimate goal and is often developed in stages by building upon previous knowledge and experience.

Conclusion

Cultural competence is not an isolated aspect of medical care, but an important component of overall excellence in health care delivery. Issues of health care quality and satisfaction are of particular concern for people with chronic conditions who frequently come into contact with the health care system. Efforts to improve cultural competence among health care professionals and organizations would contribute to improving the quality of health care for all consumers.

Guidelines From Professional Organizations Help Promote Cultural Competence

Many professional organizations representing a variety of health professionals, such as physicians, psychologists, social workers, family medicine doctors, and pediatricians have played an active role in promoting culturally competent practices through policies, research, and training efforts. For example, the American Medical Association provides information and resources on policies, publications, curriculum and training materials, and relevant activities of physician associations, medical specialty groups, and state medical societies.

Several organizations have instituted cultural competence guidelines for their memberships. For example, based on ten years of work, the Society of Teachers of Family Medicine has developed guidelines for curriculum material to teach cultural sensitivity and competence to family medicine residents and other health professionals. These guidelines focus on enhancing attitudes in the following areas:

- Awareness of the influences that sociocultural factors have on patients, clinicians, and clinical relationships.
- Acceptance of the physician's responsibility to understand the cultural aspects of health and illness
- Willingness to make clinical settings more accessible to patients
- Recognition of personal biases against people of different cultures
- Respect and tolerance for cultural differences
- Acceptance of the responsibility to combat racism, classism, ageism, sexism, homophobia, and other kinds of biases and discrimination that occur in health care settings.

Assessing Literacy Levels Can Break Down Barriers

Methods employed to assess literacy levels include the use of screening instruments that test for certain skills related to functional literacy or less formal tools that allow health care professionals to determine a person's comfort level with various modes of communication. For example, at the To Help Everyone (T.H.E.) Clinic in Los Angeles, nurses and health care professionals speak individually with patients when they arrive at the health clinic to determine whether the patient prefers to learn by using written materials, pictures, verbal counseling, or some other technique. This method of assessment allows the patient to identify their own learning style preference without having to take a literacy test; it also reduces feelings of fear or humiliation that may occur when singled out.**Federal Standards And Guidelines For Providing Culturally And Linguistically Appropriate Care**
1. The Department of Health and Human Services has provided important guidance on how to ensure culturally and linguistically appropriate health care services. The Office for Civil Rights published "Title VI Prohibition Against National Origin Discrimination as it Affects Persons with Limited English Proficiency." Very few states have developed standards for linguistic access. States that have developed such standards have focused on managed care organizations, contracting agreements with providers, and specific health and mental health services in defined settings.

2. In August 2000, the Health Care Financing Administration (now Centers for Medicare and Medicaid Services) issued guidance to all state Medicaid directors regarding interpreter and translation services, emphasizing that federal matching funds are available for states to provide oral interpretation and written translation services for Medicaid beneficiaries.

3. In December 2000, the Office of Minority Health of the Department of Health and Human Services issued 14 national standards on culturally and linguistically appropriate services (CLAS) in health care. These standards are intended to correct current inequities in the health services system and to make these services more responsive to the individual needs of all patients. They are designed to be inclusive of all cultures, with a focus on the needs of racial, ethnic, and linguistic population groups that experience unequal access to the health care system. The CLAS standards provide consistent definitions of culturally and linguistically appropriate services in health care and offer a framework for the organization and implementation of services. CLAS standards can be found at http://www.omhrc.gov/CLAS/

4. In 2002, two guides were developed to assist managed care plans with cultural and linguistically appropriate services: "Providing Oral Linguistic Services: A Guide for Managed Care Plans" and "Planning Culturally and Linguistically Appropriate Services: A Guide for Managed Care Plans." Both guides can be found at www.cms.gov/healthplans/quality/project03.asp

The Role of Community Health Workers

One such strategy is the Community Health Worker (CHW) model, which has garnered significant recognition for its progress towards health equity. Per the American Public Health Association (APHA), a CHW is "a frontline public health worker who is a trusted member of and/or has a close understanding of the community served. This trusting relationship enables the CHW to serve as a liaison/link/intermediary between health care providers and the community to facilitate access to services and improve the quality and cultural competence of service delivery."

"CHWs complement medical care delivery; with their connection to the community, CHWs can help bridge the divide between the medical system and marginalized communities."

CHWs may also be called "lay workers," "promotores de salud," "patient navigators," "community liaisons," or "peer coaches." CHWs complement medical care delivery; with their connection to the community, CHWs can help bridge the divide between the medical system and marginalized communities.

Incorporating CHWs into health care is <u>not new</u>. CHWs have been a rallying voice within the APHA since the 1970s but have recently garnered increased support and attention due to their positive impact on health equity.

How Community Health Workers Collaborate with Social Workers

CHWs and social workers have distinct yet complementary roles in supporting patients with serious illness. Some responsibilities that CHWs can fill are often excluded from health care delivery, including:

- Bridging communication between patients and their social workers, nurses, and/or physicians.
- Supporting outreach and education within specific communities (e.g., promoting health literacy, increasing the use of preventive services, and explaining the myriad social services offered by social workers).

While CHWs play an invaluable role in providing emotional support for patients and families, social workers bring the essential skills of counseling, navigating family dynamics, overcoming obstacles, and much more. CHWs improve the efficiency and effectiveness of social work by explaining its role, "translating" its benefits to improve engagement, and ensuring follow-up with community services.

Community Health Worker Roles and Responsibilities

Racial and ethnic congruence with the communities CHWs serve affords them an unparalleled understanding of cultural, linguistic, and social nuances, facilitating enhanced community engagement. In recent times, hospitals and **Federally Qualified Health Centers (FQHCs)** have hired CHWs as formal employees—and in 2010, the Bureau of Labor Statistics added CHW as an occupational code. Some colleges now offer **CHW certification and training programs** similar to public health curricula.

"Racial and ethnic congruence with the communities CHWs serve affords them an

unparalleled understanding of cultural, linguistic, and social nuances, facilitating enhanced

community engagement."

Given the diversity of a CHW's educational background, working environment, and specialty of the employer, scopes of work may vary. Using job descriptions from various FQHCs, we compiled a list of three common CHW job duties performed in patients' homes, social settings, or both:

- **Patient-Clinician Liaison:** CHWs use their community's cultural and linguistic characteristics, ensuring that health care information is communicated effectively and understood.
- **Resource Navigation**: CHWs help individuals navigate the health care system by explaining and connecting them to medical professionals, specialists, screenings, and social services based on their needs.
- **Health Education and Promotion**: CHWs provide education on health topics, disease prevention, nutrition, hygiene, and other wellness practices to individuals and

communities. They help people understand and adopt healthy behaviors in alignment with their preferences.

Example: A Community Health Worker's Role on the Palliative Care Team

An <u>expanding body of research</u> underscores the CHW's effectiveness in aiding populations that underutilize palliative care. A <u>study</u> published in 2014 found that after adding CHWs to a patient-centered medical home in the South Bronx, New York:

- Emergency department visits fell by 5%
- Hospitalizations dropped by 12.6% among patients with chronic health issues
- There was a net savings of $1,135 per patient
- There was a net savings of $170,213 annually generated by each CHW

An earlier use of CHWs occurred at <u>Harlem Hospital Center</u>, where they supported Black women when accessing mammograms and early treatment opportunities. The CHWs helped to nearly double the five-year breast cancer survival rate in that neighborhood. More recently, **CAPC completed a scan of interventions to** improve care for Black patients and families facing serious illness and identified at least 19 interventions across 15 states using CHWs. The impact of these included improved advocacy for evidence-based care and increased:

- Understanding of illness and trajectory
- Family discussions and goal alignment
- Understanding of palliative care
- Understanding of hospice
- Completion of advanced directives
- Emotional support/reduce stress

The impact of a community health worker is important and brings down costs and patients receiving services outside a hospital.

Look at the use of Financing Community Health Worker Services

Having discussed the diverse applications of CHWs, how does a palliative care team finance a CHW? It is crucial to develop a customized approach to financing that aligns with your palliative care team's specific requirements. If your team does not have the resources to hire a dedicated CHW, explore partnerships with state or community-based programs staffed by CHWs, who may extend support to patients in your shared service area. Also, many <u>state</u> **and local government websites** maintain online registries or networks where you can identify alternative avenues of support for your patients.

Additionally, teams with limited financial resources can pursue <u>grant funding</u> **opportunities** to initiate a CHW program, particularly if it would improve access to populations proven to be underserved by palliative care. Several private foundations and states endorse these program initiations due to their positive impact on advancing health equity. If you choose this route, ensure a sustainable plan is in place beyond the grant period, possibly through hospital leadership's commitment to ongoing salary support or funding through a specific value-based program.

The **2024 Medicare physician fee schedule** makes some Medicare reimbursements for patient navigation services available.

Careful Planning for Community Health Worker Integration

Lastly, if your team has the resources to integrate CHWs, you may be able to improve the overall efficiency and effectiveness of your interdisciplinary team (IDT), expanding revenue in excess of the additional salary costs. The first step that you would take is to ensure that there is a clear understanding of the CHW's scope of practice and role compared to the other positions on the IDT.

How it worked - Dr. Goldstein did this for the <u>outpatient program</u> at Mount Sinai Hospital in New York City. During an IDT retreat, his team set aside time to discuss the roles and specific responsibilities of each team member—including CHWs. They made sure to address the scope of practice and existing legal boundaries. They also discussed which responsibilities belong to the social worker and which would be appropriate for the CHWs, given the inevitable overlaps. Mapping this out helped his team identify where the overlaps lay and where handoffs should occur.

Considerations

While the CHW model is impactful, it is not without its own challenges. There is no standardized pay for CHWs, and many are often paid lower wages compared to other health care workers with similar levels of responsibility. This is a reflection of the undervaluation of their work. Additionally, low wages can make it difficult for sustainable living, leading to high turnover and reducing the quality of care provided to the patient.

Moreover, many health care organizations require a bachelor's or master's degree for CHW roles, creating a barrier for job candidates from underserved communities. With the escalating costs of college education, many people with limited financial resources find it nearly impossible to attain advanced degrees. That said, if you are hiring a CHW, consider removing the educational requirements from the job description to ensure that candidates from the underserved community of focus are not screened-out of the application process.

The Bottom Line

Community Health Workers are an effective solution to the challenges posed by a growing health care workforce shortage, an increasingly diverse patient population, and the rise in health care costs. Incorporating CHWs offers a unique opportunity to expand your team's reach in effective and more cost-efficient ways. If your organization has outpatient and community-based programs, consider adding CHWs to the team.

"Incorporating CHWs offers a unique opportunity to expand your team's reach in effective and more cost-efficient ways."

Community Health Worker (CHW) Practice Test Questions

1. The Florida Certification Board Community Health Worker (CHW) exam consists of how many questions?
    - A. 110
    - B. 200
    - C. 100
    - D. 80
2. Questions on the CHW exam cover the following topics:
    - A. Foundations of Health
    - B. Advocacy
    - C. Professional Responsibility
    - D. Resources
    - E. Community and Education
    - F. All the above
3. What is important for communication in the role of a CHW?
    - A. Listen actively
    - B. Communicate with empathy and gather information respectfully
    - C. Use language confidently and appropriately
    - D. Give information to clients and groups concisely and clearly
    - E. All the above
4. Effective communication involves identifying barriers, speaking and writing in the client's preferred language and literacy level, documenting activities, collecting data, providing feedback, and assisting in health information translation.
    - A. True
    - B. False
5. A CHW explains high blood pressure to Mrs. Jones as:
    - A. Adding 100 to your age
    - B. Circulation of more blood based on height and weight
    - C. Consulting a healthcare provider for elevated readings
    - D. Blood suddenly stopping in the brain
6. What factors put Mrs. Jones at risk for heart disease?
    - A. Using small amounts of salt, physical inactivity, being overweight
    - B. High blood pressure, high cholesterol, low blood sugar
    - C. Older age, high blood pressure, high cholesterol, diabetes, high-sodium diet
    - D. High cholesterol, low blood pressure, excessive salt use, physical inactivity
7. Cultural humility involves:
    - A. Critical self-reflection and lifelong learning
    - B. Recognizing and challenging power imbalances
    - C. Institutional accountability through respectful relationships
8. Cultural competence involves:
    - A. Awareness of one's own cultural worldview
    - B. Attitudes toward cultural differences
    - C. Knowledge of diverse cultures
    - D. Cross-cultural skills
    - E. All the above
9. Cultural competence and responsiveness include:
    - A. Understanding the role of culture in health

B. Learning culturally respectful communication
C. Using empathy for diverse backgrounds
D. Avoiding health disparities through tailored care
E. Building relationships with partners for culturally appropriate services

10. Promoting Healthy Lifestyles/HEAL includes:

A. Informing clients about healthy habits
B. Helping manage chronic illnesses
C. Improving health outcomes
D. Strengthening community connections
E. Overcoming barriers to healthy choices

11. Organizational skills include:

A. Organizing schedules, shifts, and reporting on team members and priorities to maintain clear communication
B. Planning goals for individuals and the organization considering priorities and budget
C. Establishing a safe space for coworkers with open, clear communication
D. Taking charge of event organization for workshops, outreach efforts, and educational presentations

12. Assessment skills involve all except:

A. Understanding contextual factors in assessments
B. Using formal assessment methods to engage in community initiatives
C. Designing, implementing, and interpreting community-wide assessments
D. Preparing for work shifts

13. Doulas perform all the following except:

A. Work with pregnant women
B. Serve as CHWs
C. Deliver babies
D. Perform C-sections

14. IPV stands for:

A. Intimate Partner Violence
B. Interpersonal Prevention Violence
C. Integrated Partner Values
D. International Prevention Violence

15. A CHW is not known as:

A. Health Outreach Worker
B. Promotor
C. Clinical Hospital Worker
D. Patient Navigator

16. Which is not the role of a CHW?

A. Making referrals and direct services

B. Ordering prescriptions
C. Advocating for community and individual needs
D. Health education and promotion

17. Stress can affect which organs?

A. Brain
B. Heart
C. Gut
D. All the above

18. Self-care activities include:

A. Healthy Eating
B. Physical Activity
C. Meditation
D. All the above

19. Health inequalities are defined as differences in health status between populations that are avoidable and preventable.

A. True
B. False

20. Medicaid, Childhood Insurance Programs, and Medicare are three governmental insurance programs.

A. True
B. False

21. As part of the CHW Code of Ethics, a CHW should share confidential information with relatives.

A. True
B. False

22. Ethics involves conduct and decision-making that demonstrates value and respect for people.

A. True
B. False

23. HIPAA laws are not meant to be followed.

A. True
B. False

24. HIPAA stands for the Health Insurance Portability and Accountability Act.

A. True
B. False

25. Each of the following is important in effective communication except:

A. Non-verbal communication
B. Community assessment
C. Tone of voice
D. Verbal communication

26. It is important to identify which stage of change a client is in, especially when dealing with habits like smoking or excessive alcohol consumption.

A. True
B. False

27. As a CHW, you must be mindful of privacy and confidentiality in all situations.

A. True
B. False

28. Working with clients and their personal information requires respect for their privacy, confidentiality, and their right not to share information.

A. True
B. False

29. OARS in communication stands for Open-ended questions, Affirmation, Reflective Listening, and Summarizing.

A. True
B. False

30. Ways people can experience discrimination include:

A. Healthcare
B. Education
C. Employment
D. Housing
E. All the above

31. Feelings, behavior, and thoughts are associated with mental illness or mood disorders such as depression and anxiety.

A. True
B. False

32. A CHW should be able to avoid or resolve conflicts effectively.

A. True
B. False

33. CHWs work with diverse groups and must develop positive relationships with clients, community members, supervisors, nurses, social workers, and policymakers.

A. True

B. False

34. CHWs work with diverse groups of people and must be able to develop positive relationships with clients, community members, supervisors, nurses, social workers, and policymakers.

   A. True
   B. False

35. There are four parts of Medicare: Part A, B, C, and D.

   A. True
   B. False

36. Medicare Part A covers:

   A. Inpatient hospital care, skilled nursing facility, home healthcare, and hospice
   B. Dental services, outpatient services, and physical therapy
   C. Chiropractic care, mental health services, and ambulance services
   D. Vision care, dental services, and hospice

37. Medicare Part B covers:

   A. Vision care and dental services
   B. Provider services, durable medical equipment, mental health services, preventive care, and labs
   C. Chiropractic care and inpatient services
   D. Emergency room visits and pharmacy benefits

38. Medicare Part C plans include:

   A. Health Maintenance Organization (HMO)
   B. Preferred Provider Organization (PPO)
   C. Private Fee-for-Service (PFFS)
   D. All the above

39. Medicare Part D provides coverage for:

   A. Prescription drugs
   B. Vision and dental care
   C. Physical therapy services
   D. Nursing home care

40. One in five Americans is covered by Medicare.

   A. True
   B. False

41. People generally become eligible for Medicare when they reach age 65 and have made payroll contributions to Social Security for at least 10 years.

   A. True
   B. False

42. Medicare provides coverage for people with end-stage renal disease (ESRD) and amyotrophic lateral sclerosis (ALS).

    A. True
    B. False

43. OSHA stands for the Occupational Safety and Health Administration, a federal agency under the U.S. Department of Labor.

    A. True
    B. False

44. When assisting a pregnant client, who should a CHW refer them to for prenatal care?

    A. Primary care doctor
    B. OB/GYN doctor
    C. Community health clinic
    D. Emergency room

45. OSHA's mission is to ensure safe and healthy working conditions for workers by setting and enforcing standards and providing training, outreach, education, and assistance.

    A. True
    B. False

46. The Americans with Disabilities Act (ADA) of 1990 prohibits discrimination against people with disabilities in everyday activities.

    A. True
    B. False

47. Title I of the ADA ensures that people with disabilities have access to the same employment opportunities and benefits available to people without disabilities.

    A. True
    B. False

48. Documentation for CHWs can include the following:

    A. What the community member tells you
    B. Observations from pertinent others
    C. How the community member experiences the world
    D. All the above

49. CHWs should always follow federal, state, and local laws, rules, and regulations.

    A. True
    B. False

50. CHWs should notify whom before conducting a home visit?

A. Parent
B. Cousin
C. Supervisor
D. Neighbor

51. If a CHW observes several individuals smoking marijuana outside a home they are visiting, including the patient, should they proceed with the visit?

A. Yes
B. No

52. Whom should the CHW report to in such a situation, and what should they do next?

A. Report to the sheriff's office and desk sergeant
B. Notify family members
C. Report to the supervisor and document the incident

53. Universal precautions recommend using protective barriers to reduce the risk of exposure to blood and body fluids. Examples include gloves, gowns, masks, and protective eyewear.

A. True
B. False

54. CHWs do not provide individuals with information on health and community resources or coordinate services like transportation and appointments.

A. True
B. False

55. CHWs often help patients develop care management plans and assist with scheduling appointments.

A. True
B. False

56. CHWs generally share the same language, ethnicity, socioeconomic status, and life experiences as the communities they serve.

A. True
B. False

57. CHW services should build rapport and relationships by:

A. Serving as a liaison between health services and the community
B. Increasing health knowledge and self-sufficiency through education
C. Acting as part of the care delivery team
D. Supporting and advocating for families in health services
E. All the above

58. Evidence-based strategies for using CHWs to improve healthcare access include

A. Promoting preventive behaviors

B. Providing community resources lists
C. Assisting with outreach to underserved populations
D. All the above

59. State-level support for CHWs can include:

A. Toolkits for creating partnerships
B. Maintaining a resource list for outreach
C. Supporting a statewide CHW network
D. All the above

60. CHWs conduct outreach to connect families to health insurance and primary care providers.

A. True
B. False

61. CHWs should be trained in specific diseases, healthcare systems, and community resources.

A. True
B. False

62. As care coordinators, CHWs assist individuals with complex health conditions to navigate the healthcare system.

A. True
B. False

63. CHWs help address social and non-clinical challenges that affect health outcomes.

A. True
B. False

64. CHWs can engage nontraditional partners like patients, clinicians, and policymakers to enhance community health research and reduce disparities.

A. True
B. False

65. CHWs can engage hard-to-reach individuals within vulnerable communities and advocate for their needs in research.

A. True
B. False

66. CHWs can diagnose mental health and substance use disorders without a certification and license.

A. True
B. False

67. CHWs cannot provide patients with a directory of resources or maintain and update the directory regularly.

A. True
B. False

68. CHWs are required to reconnect with patients for ongoing support or referral follow-ups.

A. True
B. False

69. CHWs should follow up on referrals to ensure appointments are kept and care is received.

A. True
B. False

70. Sharing linguistically appropriate health education materials for adults with low health literacy is part of the CHW role.

A. True
B. False

71. CHWs may conduct home visits to assess needs, offer appointment reminders, and provide health education.

A. True
B. False

72. CHWs can facilitate referrals to self-management programs, food banks, SNAP benefits, churches, and social workers.

A. True
B. False

73. If a patient loses their job and has a family with small children while applying for SNAP benefits, what should a CHW do?

A. Provide a referral to a food bank and check with a supervisor about available funds for assistance.
B. Ignore the situation as it is not part of the CHW's job.
C. Collect money from coworkers to help the family directly.

74. If a patient discloses needing help with drug use, should a CHW provide resources and referrals while consulting with their supervisor?

A. Yes
B. No

75. CHWs represent an untapped workforce capable of bridging communities with healthcare services.

A. True
B. False

76. It is not important to recognize that CHWs often join the field due to personal experiences with challenges faced by the communities they serve.

A. True
B. False

77. Adult learning is problem-centered rather than content-centered.

    A. True
    B. False

78. Adults do not need to be involved in planning and evaluating their instruction.

    A. True
    B. False

79. Adult learning experiences, including mistakes, provide the foundation for effective learning activities.

    A. True
    B. False

80. Adults are most interested in learning topics that have immediate relevance to their job or personal life.

    A. True
    B. False

81. CHW attributes or community connections include:

    A. Being a community member or having close knowledge of the community
    B. Sharing life experiences with the community
    C. A desire to help the community
    D. All the above

82. CHWs should demonstrate qualities such as maturity, persistence, creativity, resourcefulness, empathy, care, trustworthiness, and sociability.

    A. True
    B. False

83. When assessing patient barriers like transportation issues, a CHW should:

    A. Drive the patient if it's part of the CHW's duties
    B. Locate nearby public transportation options
    C. Provide taxi vouchers or transit tickets
    D. All the above

84. CHWs play integral roles in clinical, public health, and social systems, serving in maternal and child health, chronic disease intervention, immunization, oral health, and other areas.

    A. True
    B. False

85. CHWs have been recognized for addressing racial equity and social determinants of health by connecting individuals to basic needs and reducing health disparities.

A. True
B. False

86. CHWs often teach clients how to prepare heart-healthy meals, increase physical activity, quit smoking, and assess crises for further support.

   A. True
   B. False

87. CHWs help patients understand their rights to healthcare and social services and advocate for individual and community health needs.

   A. True
   B. False

88. CHWs help bridge cultural differences between communities and healthcare or social service systems.

   A. True
   B. False

89. When a non-English speaking community member from Spain needs help, a CHW should seek assistance from:

   A. A French-speaking interpreter
   B. A Chinese-speaking interpreter
   C. A Spanish-speaking interpreter

90. Ethics are not essential for CHWs, and they can make decisions without following organizational policies.

   A. True
   B. False

91. CHWs should always follow universal precautions, OSHA standards, and personal protective measures.

   A. True
   B. False

92. CHWs should collect and use data to identify and respond to community strengths and needs.

   A. True
   B. False

93. CHWs should use strategies that promote positive behavioral outcomes, such as identifying resources, making referrals, following up, and monitoring progress.

   A. True
   B. False

94. CHWs are only expected to behave professionally during office hours and can act without following ethical guidelines during home visits.

A. Not at all
B. Always
C. Only in the office

95. To apply for certification with the Florida Certification Board, a CHW must have completed 30 hours of training and have no supervised work experience.

A. True
B. False

96. The content covered in the required 30 hours of CHW training is not necessary if the applicant has previous nursing assistant experience.

A. True
B. False

97. To prevent burnout, CHW supervisors should manage workload, support healthy boundaries, and provide continuing education.

A. True
B. False

98. Organizations may provide CHWs with mobile devices such as cell phones or tablets for home visits to enhance safety and monitoring.

A. True
B. False

99. The Medicaid and CHIP State Plan describes the services offered under a state's Medicaid and Children's Health Insurance Program.

A. True
B. False

100. Medicaid Managed Care requires actuarial soundness, including which of the following?

A. Service costs
B. Administrative expenses
C. Both A & B
D. None of the above

Community Health Worker (CHW) Practice Test Answer Key

1. C
2. F (All the above)
3. E (All the above)
4. True
5. C
6. C
7. True
8. E (All the above)
9. True
10. True
11. True
12. 6 (Drive to work prepared for clocking in for shift)
13. D (Perform a C-section)
14. True
15. C (Clinical Hospital Worker)
16. B (Order prescriptions)
17. True
18. D (All the above)
19. True
20. True
21. False
22. True
23. False
24. True
25. B (Community Assessment)
26. True
27. True
28. True
29. True
30. F (All the above)
31. True
32. True
33. F (All the above)
34. True
35. True
36. A
37. B
38. D (All the above)
39. A
40. True
41. True
42. True
43. True
44. B (OB/GYN Doctor)
45. True
46. True
47. True
48. D (All the above)
49. False

50. C (Supervisor)
51. B (No)
52. C (Supervisor and document)
53. True
54. False
55. True
56. True
57. E (All the above)
58. D (All the above)
59. D (All the above)
60. True
61. True
62. True
63. True
64. True
65. True
66. False
67. False
68. False
69. True
70. True
71. True
72. True
73. A (Provide referral to Food Bank and check with supervisor about funds to initiate help)
74. A (Yes)
75. True
76. False
77. True
78. False
79. True
80. True
81. D (All the above)
82. True
83. D (All the above)
84. True
85. True
86. True
87. True
88. True
89. C (Spanish-speaking interpreter)
90. False
91. True
92. True
93. True
94. A (Not at all)
95. False
96. False
97. True
98. True
99. True
100. C (Both A & B)

Certification Requirements	Minimum Requirements
Formal Education	High School Diploma or General Equivalency Degree High School Diplomas or General Equivalence Degrees must be eligible for acceptance by colleges or universities holding nationally recognized accreditation through the United States Department of Education and/or Council on Higher Education Accreditation (CHEA).
Content Specific Training	30 hours of content specific training, allocated as follows: 1. Communication and Education: 4 hours 2. Resources: 4 hours 3. Advocacy: 4 hours 4. Foundations of Health: 4 hours 5. Professional Responsibility: 4 hours 6. Electives: 10 hours Eligible training must be taken from an FCB Approved Education Provider within the last 10 years (no time limit on college coursework taken as part of a degree program). FCB Eligible Training Guidelines and Providers are listed online on FCB's website www.flcertificationboard.org under Education & Training. Content specific training and supporting documentation is submitted to the FCB by the applicant. Applicants must complete (1) The FCB Training Verification Form and (2) Attach approved supporting documentation for each entry listed on the Form.
Related Work Experience	500 hours of work and/or volunteer experience providing community health worker services in any of the following domains of practice: • Communication and Education: tasks related to community education • Resources: tasks related to linking community members with available health/social services • Advocacy: tasks related to advocating for the community's health/social service needs Work/volunteer experience must be directly related to the core competencies of the credential and must have occurred within the last 5 years
FCB Recommendations	Three (3) professional letters of recommendation for certification.
FCB Exam	Certified Community Health Worker Exam – 100 questions
CEU- Continuing Education	10 hours per year. Training content must be related to at least one of the CCHW performance domains as indicated under Content Specific Training. Continuing Education (CE) credit hours must be non-repetitive (i.e., the same course cannot be claimed more than one time during each credentialed period, even if the course is taken annually).

Certification Renewal	Biennial (every two years), on October 31st of the renewal year

The Florida Certification Board also requires a Level II background check.

FCB policy requires all applicants to pass a Level 2 Background Screening that is conducted through the Department of Children and Families. FCB will initiate background checks for individuals seeking the CCHW credential. Regardless of if you have been previously approved for a FCB credential or DCF Level 2 Background, you must complete and return the Clearinghouse Applicant Request Form and Privacy Policy Form.

The length of time for an application to be approved depends on the timeliness and quality of the documents received by the FCB. We strongly recommend that you ensure you understand the certification process and create a plan to complete all steps before completing/submitting either of the online applications.

Hard copy applications are only available for applicants who meet ADA requirements related to accommodations for using computers and related technologies. Please contact the FCB for additional assistance.

CREATE AN ONLINE ACCOUNT

All applicants MUST first establish an online account with the FCB. Please go to our website at www.flcertificationboard.org and click on My Account to access the portal.

- If you have an account, simply login.

- If this is your first time working with the FCB, click on the My Account link to create a new account.

- If you have forgotten your login or password, please call the office. DO NOT CREATE MULTIPLE ACCOUNTS.

CREATE AN ONLINE APPLICATION FOR CERTIFICATION

Applicants will be required to complete an online application.

CCHW Application: Once you have access to your online account, select the "Apply for New Certification" button and then select the **Certified Community Health Worker** application. See the CCHW Online Application Components and Submission Protocol section of this document for additional details.

An application is considered submitted when the applicant has progressed through all of the screens, providing all system required information, and making the application fee payment.

- You can access the application for a maximum of 45 days. Applications not submitted within 45 days will be automatically deleted, including all data and attachments.

- Once the application is submitted and the fee payment is received, the application is "locked." This means that the applicant can no longer make changes to data entered into the application and cannot add additional files of supporting documentation. Please work directly with your assigned Certification Specialist, who will make the necessary changes/updates.

DOWNLOAD AND DISTRIBUTE/COMPLETE REQUIRED FORMS

All credential-specific requirements are documented on FCB forms. All forms are posted online, under Credentials at FCB's website, www.flcertificationboard.org. All forms must be filled out electronically – handwritten forms will be denied.

All forms and supporting documentation must be submitted to the FCB by the individual signing off on the form/submitting supporting documentation. Forms and documents provided by the applicant will be denied.

All hard copy documents and fee payments may be made to the FCB via mail, email or fax to (850) 222-6247. US Mail: FCB ω 1715 South Gadsden Street ω Tallahassee, Florida, 32301

Email: Applicants are assigned a Certification Specialist when their application has been received at the FCB. Please ask the applicant for their Certification Specialist's name and email address. In the absence of a specified person, FCB accepts email at admin_assist@flcertificationboard.org.

Resources

- Florida Certification Board: Certified Community Health Worker (https://flcertificationboard.org/certifications/certified-community-health-worker/)
- Center to Advance Palliative Care: Enhancing Care for Diverse Communities (https://www.capc.org/blog/enhancing-care-for-diverse-communities-the-role-of-community-health-workers/)
- Social Security Administration: Medicare Plan Parts (https://www.ssa.gov/medicare/plan/medicare-parts)
- Americans with Disabilities Act: Introduction to ADA (https://www.ada.gov/topics/intro-to-ada/)
- Occupational Safety and Health Administration: OSHA (https://www.osha.gov/)
- Health Equity Tracker: What is Health Equity? (https://healthequitytracker.org/whatishealthequity)
- Health.gov: Social Determinants of Health (https://health.gov/healthypeople/priority-areas/social-determinants-health)
- The American Association of Community Health Workers: Code of Ethics (https://health.mo.gov/professionals/community-health-workers)
- Centers for Medicare & Medicaid Services: Medicare Learning Network (https://www.cms.gov/outreach-and-education/medicare-learning-network-mln)
- Western Governors University: Adult Learning Theories and Principles (https://www.wgu.edu/blog/adult-learning-theories-principles2004.html)
- National Center for Biotechnology Information: Community Health Workers Research (https://www.ncbi.nlm.nih.gov/pmc/articles/PMC3477991/)
- Florida CHW Coalition: FL CHW Coalition (https://www.flchwcoalition.org/)
- World Health Organization: Social Determinants of Health (https://www.who.int/health-topics/social-determinants-of-health#tab=tab_1)
- Georgetown University: Cultural Competency (https://hpi.georgetown.edu/cultural/)
- Target HIV: Cross-Cultural Skills (https://targethiv.org/sites/default/files/supporting-files/chw-cc-05-Cross-Cultural-Skills.pdf)
- Centers for Disease Control and Prevention: Universal Precautions (https://www.cdc.gov/mmwr/preview/mmwrhtml/00000039.htm)
- Minnesota CHW Alliance: CHW Role in Health Equity (https://mnchwalliance.org/role-of-chws-in-health-equity/)
- Massachusetts Government: Triple Aim Success with CHWs (https://www.mass.gov/doc/achieving-the-triple-aim-success-with-community-health-workers0/download)
- Rural Health Information Hub: CHW Toolkits and Resources (https://www.ruralhealthinfo.org/toolkits/community-health-workers/2/manager)
- Rural Health Information Hub: Project Examples (https://www.ruralhealthinfo.org/project-examples/911)
- National Heart, Lung, and Blood Institute: Role of CHWs (https://www.nhlbi.nih.gov/health/educational/healthdisp/role-of-community-healthworkers.htm)
- Centers for Disease Control and Prevention: States Implementing CHW Strategies (https://www.cdc.gov)
- Cambridge University Press: Enhancing Community Engagement (https://www.cambridge.org)
- PCORI: Expanding CHW Home Visit Program (https://www.pcori.org)
- Centers for Medicare & Medicaid Services: On the Front Lines of Health Equity (https://www.cms.gov)
- Florida Health: CHW Use and Access to Healthcare (https://www.floridahealth.gov/programs-and-services/minority-health/CommunityResources/CHWUseandAccesstoHealthcare.pdf)

Made in United States
Orlando, FL
19 March 2025